*Then the Lord looked
upon the earth, and filled it
with His blessings.
Sirach 16:27*

The intent and
purpose of this volume is to
give you faith, hope and inspira-
tion. Hopefully it will help bring peace
and tranquility into your life. May it be a
reminder of God's love, guidance
and His many blessings.

Our publications help to support our work
for needy children in over 120 countries
around the world. Through our
programs, thousands of children are
fed, clothed, educated, sheltered
and given the opportunity to
live decent lives.

Salesian Missions wishes to extend special thanks and gratitude to our generous poet friends and to the publishers who have given us permission to reprint material included in this book. Every effort has been made to give proper acknowledgments. Any omissions or errors are deeply regretted, and the publisher, upon notification, will be pleased to make the necessary corrections in subsequent editions.

First Edition Printed in the U.S.A. by Concord Litho Group, Concord, New Hampshire 03301.

Blessings
Upon Blessings
from the Salesian Collection

Compiled and edited by
Jennifer Grimaldi

Illustrated by
Dale Begley, Russell Bushée,
Frank Massa, Maureen McCarthy,
Gail Pepin, Paul Scully,
and Robert Van Steinburg

Contents

The Aisle of Springtime

Come, walk the aisle of Spring
In God's cathedral, earth;
Look up and see the azure skies
And witness earth's rebirth:

The springing flow'rs, the buzzing bees,
The birds in choral song;
The greening grasses on display,
The budding leaves so young.

Come, tread the aisle of springtime,
Gold-paved with dandelion
And see God's great cathedral, earth,
At this renewal time.

Loise Pinkerton Fritz

A Glimpse of Spring

I caught a glimpse of Spring today
As Winter tiptoed on her way.
There still was ice and snow around,
But pushing up through frozen ground
Were crocuses so brave and dear,
Proclaiming springtime was quite near.
A lovely sight you are, you know,
Gold flowers shining in the snow;
God's choice for ushering in the Spring,
Gladness and hope to us you bring.
Assuring us of life anew
When every Winter storm is through.

Beverly J. Anderson

A Spring World

May is a Spring world,
Elusive and bright,
The magic of fragrance,
The beauty of light,
The sensory season
With grass reaching tall,
Trees leaf in wonder,
Sunbeams now fall.

May is a Spring world,
Soft climbing hills,
Meadows and birdsong,
Gay whippoorwills,

Nature so friendly,
Vibrant – alive,
Butterflies winging,
Bees in their hives.

Beautiful Spring child,
Orchard aglow,
Blossoms now tingle,
Soft breezes blow,
God in His Heaven,
Hearts that can dream,
Wonderful Maytime,
A Spring world supreme.

Garnett Ann Schultz

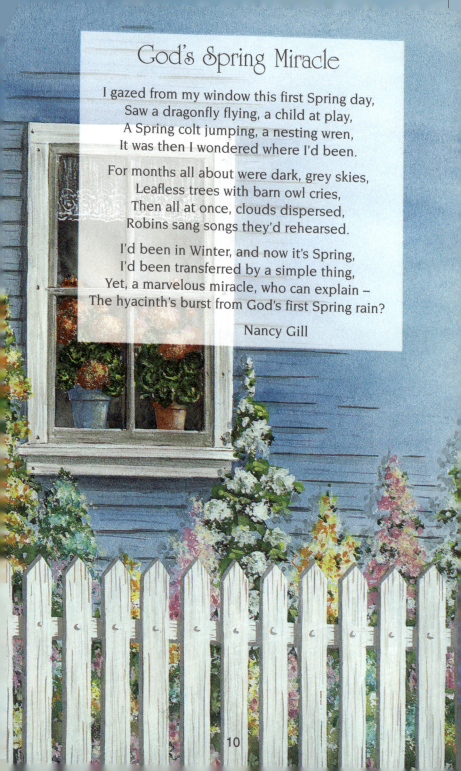

God's Spring Miracle

I gazed from my window this first Spring day,
Saw a dragonfly flying, a child at play,
A Spring colt jumping, a nesting wren,
It was then I wondered where I'd been.

For months all about were dark, grey skies,
Leafless trees with barn owl cries,
Then all at once, clouds dispersed,
Robins sang songs they'd rehearsed.

I'd been in Winter, and now it's Spring,
I'd been transferred by a simple thing,
Yet, a marvelous miracle, who can explain –
The hyacinth's burst from God's first Spring rain?

Nancy Gill

God Made Them All

God made the ocean,
God made the stream,
Each wonderful hilltop,
The valleys in between.
He sent us the springtime
With flowers so bright
And added the starshine
To brighten the night.
God loaned a rainbow
After life's storm
And sent us the sunshine,
All lovely and warm,
The colors of Autumn,
Each soft drop of rain,
The blue skies above us,
Each meadow and plain.
The green grass of Maytime,
Each flower grown wild,
The laughter of raindrops,
The love of a child,
A world filled with beauty,
The magic of Fall,
Each smile and each blessing –
God made them all.

Garnett Ann Schultz

This is the day the Lord has made;
let us be glad and rejoice in it.
Psalm 118:24

The River, the Wind and the Birds

When Spring arrives I feel the urge
To do ought else than sing;
With witness to the awakenings
This season always brings.

The river now begins to flow,
Once covered with thick ice;
To deluge my soul with gladness,
Its music doth suffice.

To be again in touch with earth
In planting garden seeds;
And sowing in the new-plowed fields
Supplies my spirit food it needs.

To these are added accents
Of music from the birds;
The rites they sing I must confess
To be the sweetest I have heard.

The winds that blow this time of year,
Too, add their special note;
I join them in their prayer and praise,
God's strength and courage to invoke.

For Spring comes as a busy time,
Yet is filled with joy and mirth
And displays the accomplished promise
Of a new, refreshing birth.

Don Beckman

How great are Your works,
O Lord! How profound
Your purpose!
Psalm 92:6

God Is Always There

Lord, don't let me get caught up
In another busy day
That I can't find some special time
To talk with You and pray.
To thank You for the little things
That You send to me each day,
A voice of joy, a touch of love
To spread along life's way.
Send Your blessings forth from me
To help one soul in pain,
And if I use the gifts You send,
I shall not have lived in vain.
Oh, how my soul thirsts for You.
Your love is beyond compare.
What a comfort it is to know
That You are always there.

Shirley Hile Powell

Begin Each Day With Prayer

Begin each day with prayer, my friend,
While everything is new,
With scarlet ribbons in the sky
And the roses fresh with dew.

Each day is filled with miracles
For those who do God's will.
He greets us with the sunrise
When all is bright and still.

He speaks to those who listen
For we are set apart
To honor Him in all we do
And hold Him in our heart.

Begin each day with prayer, my friend,
For strength comes from above,
Then rise and shine throughout the day,
Reflecting His great love.

Clay Harrison

June's Many Charms

The hillsides are aglow with June,
The meadows, bright and fair,
Adorned with clover, Queen Anne's lace
And daisies everywhere.

The sunshine's warm upon my face,
I feel a gentle breeze.
Sunbeams are playing peek-a-boo
With lacy cherry trees.

Each rose garden's a masterpiece –
A wondrous work of art.
Their colors are so glorious –
How they uplift my heart.

There's birdsong everywhere I go,
The grass is lush and green.
Soft skies of azure blue shine down
Upon June's charming scene.

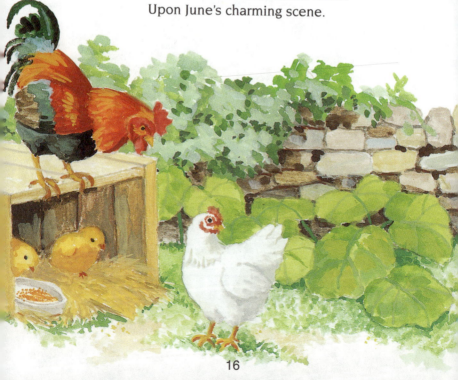

This is a time for dreaming hearts,
June has so much to share.
She beckons me to walk her trails
And leave behind all care.

Here mid-June's beauty unsurpassed,
Her quiet, gentle ways,
I find a peace and sweet content
And bow my head in praise.

I thank God for such days as these,
Aglow with many charms,
Where happiness is mine to hold
While nestled in June's arms.

Beverly J. Anderson

*Bless the Lord, all His works, everywhere in
His domain. Bless the Lord, O my soul!*
Psalm 103:22

Through Love-Smiling Eyes

I want to see life through the eyes of a child
And live with its love in my heart,
And see all the gladness and beauty of life
That a child enjoys and imparts;
I want to be happy, contented and pleased
With the common-found treasures of earth,
And to live with the trust and faith of a child
God wills to His children at birth.

I want to see joy in all of God's works
That a child enjoys every day,
And the magic of laughter that brightens each nook
Where a child finds rapture in play;
And I want to see love – to harvest and sow –
That a child gives away with a smile;
And to count my blessings and treasures in life
Through the love-smiling eyes of a child.

Michael Dubina

Make Me Worthy

As I walk along life's road,
Please, God, never let me be
Travelling at such a pace
That I can't find time for Thee.

Nor let me gaze upon a flower
And breathe the sweet, clean air
Without a special thanks to Thee
For having put them there.

Let me not pass others by,
However they might live –
There may be those who could use
Some love that I can give.

Help to lift upon my shoulders
Half of someone's heavy load,
Then, dear God, please make me worthy
To walk down life's winding road!

Doris A. Orth

*Heaven is the Heaven of the
Lord, but the earth He has
given to the children of men.*
Psalm 115:16

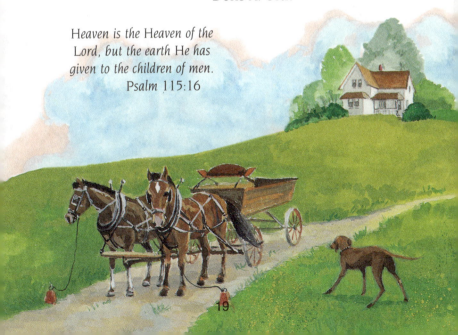

19

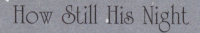

How Still His Night

How still His night that settles in;
How soft His breezes blow
Upon this scene: a closing pause –
This time I cherish so.
A hectic day of problems that
Create the face of care;
How still His night that settles in –
I'm glad that He is there.

God brings us pause to bring us rest
In softer shades of night;
Reflective times to ponder on
His ever-guiding light.
How still His night that settles in;
How strong His beacon's glare;
And I am wont to offer praise –
Safe in His loving care.

Henry W. Gurley

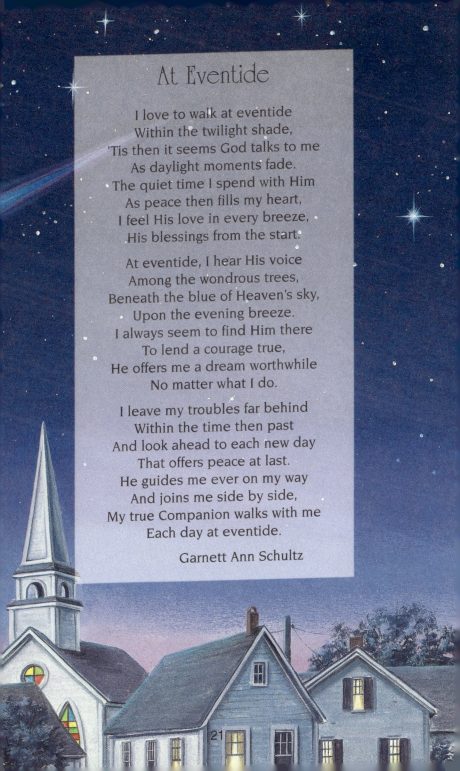

At Eventide

I love to walk at eventide
Within the twilight shade,
'Tis then it seems God talks to me
As daylight moments fade.
The quiet time I spend with Him
As peace then fills my heart,
I feel His love in every breeze,
His blessings from the start.

At eventide, I hear His voice
Among the wondrous trees,
Beneath the blue of Heaven's sky,
Upon the evening breeze.
I always seem to find Him there
To lend a courage true,
He offers me a dream worthwhile
No matter what I do.

I leave my troubles far behind
Within the time then past
And look ahead to each new day
That offers peace at last.
He guides me ever on my way
And joins me side by side,
My true Companion walks with me
Each day at eventide.

Garnett Ann Schultz

21

God's Masterpiece

There is a stir of excitement
That is felt in Autumn air.
An abundance of spectacular color
Seems to be scattered everywhere.

Oh, how our God must love us;
He fills your earth and mine
With the miracles of His wonders
In the season of autumntime.

The flaming hills are all alive
With leaves of gold and red.
The ground is covered with fallen leaves
Down the paths on which we tread.

The scattered frost in mornings
Reminds us that Winter is near,
But let us enjoy the beauty
Of God's masterpiece this year.

Shirley Hile Powell

Hills and Mountains of Life

Many are the hills and mountains
We must challenge on this earth
With the will that God endowed us
To enhance our holy birth;
Hills and mountains we must conquer –
To enjoy the other side –
Where our dreams and hopes and fortunes
Hold more promise to provide.

And we sweat and strive and struggle
To surmount each rocky hill
With a lot of tears and anguish
To achieve what hope instills,
But we never quit in trying
Or shun a daring climb
If the other side holds promise
Of a life that's more sublime.

Michael Dubina

Splendor and majesty go before Him;
praise and joy are in His holy place.
1 Chronicles 16:27

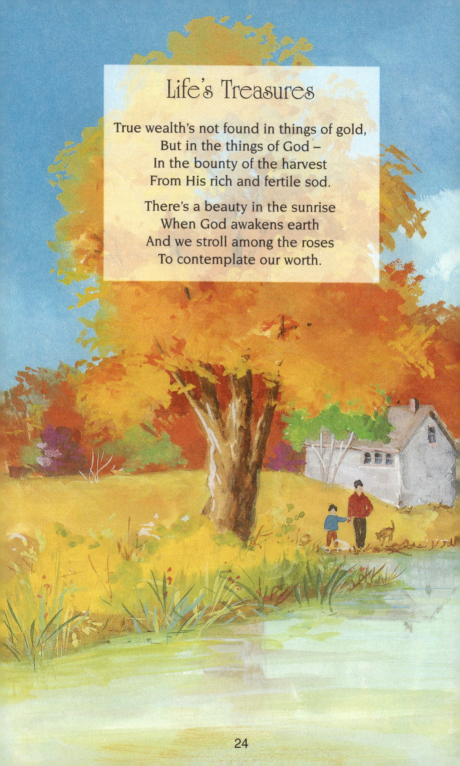

Life's Treasures

True wealth's not found in things of gold,
But in the things of God –
In the bounty of the harvest
From His rich and fertile sod.

There's a beauty in the sunrise
When God awakens earth
And we stroll among the roses
To contemplate our worth.

There are moments soft and tender
Shared with friends and family
That sustain us through the hard times
By just their memory.

There are moments truly golden
As through the years we trod
When we learn that all our blessings
Are treasures sent by God.

Clay Harrison

25

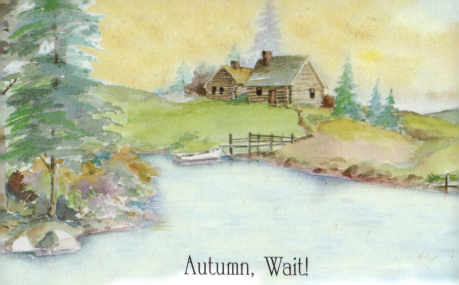

Autumn, Wait!

Don't leave so soon, oh, Autumn, wait,
We've yet so many hills to climb,
So much to see, so much to share,
And we have had so little time.
Oh Autumn, wait, your memories
Can soothe the lonely heart that grieves,
It's been so long since I have walked
Down winding lanes of golden leaves.

I've missed the sweet serenity
That follows grey November rain,
October's ombre sunsets splashed
Across the leaden skies again.
The shadowed flames beyond the grate,
Where firelight flickers… Autumn, wait!

Grace E. Easley

He causes the changes of the times and
seasons, makes kings and unmakes
them. He gives wisdom to the wise and
knowledge to those who understand.
Daniel 2:21

Belief in Him

I learned to know Him very young,
I did not have to see
His blessed face for Him to be
So very real to me.
I found I could depend on Him,
And as the years go by,
There is a special kind of love
Between the Lord and I.
There is no room within my soul
For bitterness or doubt,
And in my heart the firm belief
God knows what He's about.
I know sometimes I grow depressed
When storm clouds hide the sun,
But then His voice, "I'll care for you,
The way I've always done."
And suddenly, the shadows fade
And I am reassured,
And everything that bothered me,
His loving hands have cured.
Perhaps the things that I profess
Are not those you would choose,
But never challenge me on faith
…For you would surely lose.

Grace E. Easley

God Holds the Blueprint

On this vast earth on which we live,
We're but a speck of sand,
Yet God knows each of us by name,
It is the way He planned.

In awe, we view His wondrous works
On sod and sea and sky
And marvel at His handiwork,
The how, the when, the why.

Yet, He is not beyond our reach –
He hears the faintest prayer,
And deep within our hearts we feel
His love beyond compare.

How majestic is our God,
How fearsome His power,
And still how gentle is this One
Who comforts in darkest hour.

Man strives to prove his theories,
How creation came to be,
But God alone holds the blueprint
No mortal eyes can see.

Kay Hoffman

How varied are Your works, O Lord!
In wisdom You have wrought them all —
the earth is full of Your creatures.
Psalm 104:24

God's as Close as a Prayer

I'll carry a pocket of sunbeams
For a dark, dreary day.
Memory's garden will blossom
When Winter comes my way!

I'll see all of the flowers
Growing on the cliffs of despair
And those things will remind me
God's as close as a prayer!

Dottlee Duggan Reid

Help Me, Lord

Help me, Lord, if I should stumble
And my feet should go astray;
Or foolishly I wander
And perhaps should lose my way.

Help me, Lord, if I'm unkind
Or not as loving as I should,
Or if sometimes foolish motives
Keep me back from doing good.

Help me, Lord, to trust You more
And in Your love to feel secure,
So if trials should come my way,
All things then I can endure.

Olive B. Elvin

Help me, O Lord, my God;
save me, in Your kindness.
Psalm 109:26

Friends

I wish that words would come to me
That I might say to you –
For all that you have meant to me,
For times you've seen me through.
You have given me so much
That I could not repay,
The joy, the peace, the strengthening light
To brighten up my day.
You've shown me just what it means
To trust in God above,
To rest my weary soul in Him,
To feel His gracious love.
You've helped me with each burden
That seemed so hard to bear,
You've taught me how to face each day,
You've guided me with care.
And if I may express my thoughts
That are known to God above,
To give you just a portion
Of the deepness of my love.

To let you know just how I feel,
Just what you mean to me,
To see the smile upon your face,
To enjoy your company.
And as the days grow shorter
When there's still so much to do,
I'd like to take this moment now
To say these words to you:
You'll never be forgotten,
You'll always walk with me,
I'll cherish all the love you gave
In each sweet memory.
I'll say a prayer of thanks to God
For sending you my way,
That He will bless your every step
To guide you every day.
And when new problems I must face,
Which I'll so often do,
I'll close my eyes and say a prayer –
Then I'll remember you.

Debbie Hiber

Half as Sweet

Though Winter's sun is half as sweet
As is the sun of May,
I love its throbbing touch upon
A cold and wintry day.

The blankets of snow and ice
Perforce must go away;
But I shall cherish most this time
And watch the children play…

Upon the hills of sparkling snow –
On sled, on slide, on sleigh –
Their gleeful laughter on the air
On this sweet Winter's day.

Henry W. Gurley

Winter Will Pass

Winter will pass and roses will bloom,
Sunshine will sparkle and brighten your room.
Raindrops of April will bless Maytime flowers
When magical moments are then quickly ours.
Gardens will blossom and lawns will turn green,
Bright sparkling bubbles will top every stream.

Winter will pass, we know, oh, so sure
That blue skies above us will truly endure.
Springtime's rich beauties – contentment our own –
And we'll find a blessing we've not before known.
The season of wonder – of planting the soil,
The joy of fulfillment in days filled with toil.

One moment of laughter – another of bliss,
A sweet, tiny angel will offer a kiss.
God's miracles real that forever abound
While hearts then delight to each sight and each sound,
The snow now is melted – we've sunbeams at last
Because God assures us the Winter will pass.

Garnett Ann Schultz

Frustrations

Sometimes it seems that Nature gives
Us wings to fly away,
But then it takes away our sky
And we on earth must stay.

Frustrations come to test our faith,
Sometimes we're overcome,
But then an angel draws so near
And we begin to hum.

And from our humming comes a song
And from the song comes mirth,
Then really it is not so bad
To be confined to earth.

We're diamonds in the rough, my friends,
And we must polished be
So when frustrations come our way,
Dear God, we'll look to Thee.

For with each trial comes the strength
To overcome the foe
And if we daily trust in God,
We'll win the race, I know!

Luther Elvis Albright

*But I pray to You, Lord, for the time of
Your favor. God, in Your great kindness
answer me with Your constant help.*
Psalm 69:14

Dazzling Spring

Springtime bursts upon the scene
In a gown of emerald green.
I opened up my door to greet
Purple lilacs at my feet.

Then a charming chickadee
Sang his song from the apple tree.
Creatures of the woodland wild
Frolicked like a frisky child.

April showers came to drench
Ivy 'twining 'round my bench.
Said God, "I think I'll spread some mirth,"
And sunbeams dazzled Mother Earth.

Nora M. Bozeman

The Hope of Spring

Gentle rain and glistening dew
Give life to barren Winter sod.
A springtime tulip opens wide
And raises petaled eyes to God.

Trees are gowned in lacy green;
Springtime displays her lovely frills.
The hills are standing tall and proud
And turning gold with daffodils.

God extends His gentle hand
To each sleepy, hibernating thing;
For the Winter never leaves us
Without the hope of Spring.

Barbara Cagle Ray

*May Your kindness, Lord, be upon us;
we have put our hope in You.*
Psalm 33:22

Bless This, Our Home

Bless this, our little home, dear Lord,
And fill it with Your love
And keep us ever-mindful of
Your blessings from above.

Give to each room old-fashioned charm
And warm the heart with cheer
That all who come and gather 'round
Will find glad welcome here.

Watch o'er our little children, Lord,
So happy at their play
And keep them safe within Your care
And hear them when they pray.

Help us to be good parents
In a world where much is wrong
That they will learn true values here,
A faith that's sure and strong.

Make of our home a blessing, Lord,
With door swung open wide –
A haven for a friend or stranger
Where love dwells inside.

Kay Hoffman

*The Lord bless you
and keep you!*
Numbers 6:24

41

Greatest Joys of Life

Our greatest joys of love and life
That fill the heart with grace
Are kindly deeds we do each day
That Jesus will embrace.
For these kindnesses of care
We plead for – in our prayers –
And cry for – in our times of need –
To help us from despair.

A deed of love or simple care
For those who cry in need
Is what the Lord expects of us
In acts of Christian deeds;
And He will bless us in return
With joys of Christian heart
For every gift we give away
That love and care impart.

Michael Dubina

Cherished
Friendship Days

As time goes by, our friendship days
Hold memories to recall,
We learn to value each day's joys,
We treasure them, one and all.

We know the strength a friend can bring
Through happy times or tears,
And life becomes more enriching
In friendship's inspiring years.

Our friendships like a mirror shine,
Reflecting our trust and love.
Those dear, remembered, keepsake days –
Life's precious gifts from God above.

Elisabeth Weaver Winstead

*All good giving and every
perfect gift is from above…*
James 1:17

My Little Part of the World

It's my little part of a great, big world,
Perhaps such a tiny share,
And yet it is home – the place that I love
Where I kneel in a whispered prayer.
I've lived here through all of the years just past,
Through troubles and heartaches and strife,
The happiness and the million dreams
That add meaning true to my life.

My little part of the world so vast,
Shining meadows – each tree that I love,
I own that so beautiful hill afar
And the stars that shine down from above.

Just a quaint farmhouse in quietness here,
Nothing fancy and surely not great,
But it holds the treasures of yesterdays past –
'Tis here that I always shall rate.

The others so precious have now come and gone,
Yet leaving such memories dear,
Each bright, shining face and each loving heart
Still lend magic moments of cheer.
And I call it mine – the farmhouse of old,
The so tiny treasures unfurled.
I ask for so little – just happiness, love –
In my own little part of the world.

Garnett Ann Schultz

A Shelter for My Soul

Though storm clouds may overwhelm me
And tempests billow my sails –
Though I may stray from my charted course,
There's a beacon that never fails.
It penetrates the night and the darkness,
Leading me from the rocky shoal –
And in the chasm of my heart,
There's a shelter for my soul.
He's the Captain of my journey,
He's my Pilot on a wind-swept sea,
He's the Savior of my troubled soul
And He's there to sail with me.

Dorothy C. Deitz

Footprints

Although I leave my footprints in
The sands of time, I know
That rains will wash, that winds will dry
And make them dimmer grow.

But may they never be erased
Completely and may they
Serve as a path for some to tread
While on their upward way.

And if I deviate and walk
Along the ways of sin,
May time quite soon erase those prints
So none can walk therein.

Luther Elvis Albright

*You restoreth my strength. You
guide me along the right path
for the sake of Your name.*
Psalm 23:3

47

We Never Fail

We never fail unless we quit –
No longer seek and strive,
Unless we then refuse to try
To keep our hopes alive.
If we keep faith within our soul
And laughter in our heart,
However difficult our path,
We'll find a bright, new start.

We never fail, however rough
The road ahead might seem;
We've but to ever still keep on
To realize our dream.
'Tis only quitters who give up,
Complaining as they go,
We've only to accept the fact
We reap just what we sow.

The world awaits courageous souls
Who ever give their best,
Through every trial that is their own
Sometimes a rich success.
We've but to know that God alone
Still guides the ship we sail
And if we reach and take His hand,
For sure, we'll never fail.

Garnett Ann Schultz

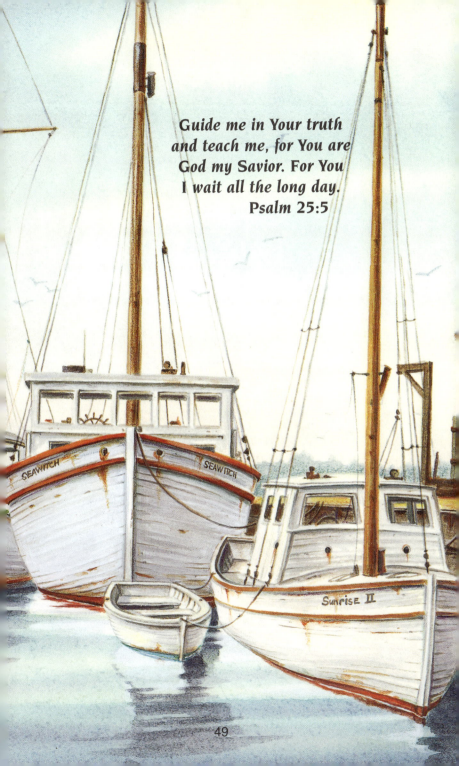

Guide me in Your truth
and teach me, for You are
God my Savior. For You
I wait all the long day.
Psalm 25:5

An Invitation

The church bells echo o'er the land
Upon this holy day,
Calling families to church
To worship and to pray.
To cast aside all earthly cares
That warp the troubled mind,
And bow to God in simple trust,
A God who's just and kind.
To sing His praises loud and long,
To meditate in prayer;
The church bells sound for you and me
As God awaits us there.

Loise Pinkerton Fritz

50

I Hear Thee Knocking...

I hear Thee knocking, precious Master,
I hear Thee knocking at my door;
I hear Thee knocking, oh, my Savior,
As I have heard Thee times before.

I hear Thee knocking, precious Master;
I need Thee more than e'er before;
I thank Thee for Thy love and caring –
Please come and enter through my door.

I hear Thee knocking, precious Master;
I need Thy love and strength once more,
For I am weak and heavy laden –
Come, Lord, and enter through my door.

I hear Thee knocking, precious Master;
Please take away my pain and fear;
My heart and soul are Thine, dear Savior,
Oh, come and stay forever near!

Hope C. Oberhelman

*Know that the Lord works
wonders for the faithful; the
Lord hears when I call out.*
Psalm 4:4

Autumn's Grand Finale

Linger with us, dear Autumn.
Don't be so quick to leave,
For when you bid a fond farewell,
I know my heart shall grieve.

I love to wade in shallow streams
In the warmth of Autumn's sun
And walk among the painted hills
Until the day is done.

The harvest moon that hangs so low
Always takes my breath away,
Yet I yearn for the light of morning
To cherish another Autumn day.

The birds are getting restless;
They know it is time to fly
To the warmth of southern places
Across the brilliant azure sky.

We are blessed with a grand finale
As God sends us one last show.
He fills the earth with Autumn's colors
Before the coming Winter's snow.

Shirley Hile Powell

Signs of Autumn

Fall, once more, has descended –
There's a briskness in the air!
Beds of pungent, Autumn flowers
Emit their fragrance everywhere.

Trees are changing all their colors –
Hues of red and gold are found.
Leaves are making earth's new carpet,
Slowly spreading o'er the ground.

Soon old Winter will be calling
With his early morning chill;
But for now, let's savor Autumn –
While it lingers, soft and still.

Mary S. Chevalier

One Moment's Time

If I could have one moment's time
That I could truly claim as mine,
This lovely, bright September day
Before the Summer fades away,
One crowning hour – 'midst skies of blue
While gentle breezes whisper through.

One moment's time at Summer's end,
The loveliness that gardens lend,
The marigolds and dahlias, too,
With rainbow asters peeking through,
A last red rose that's blooming there,
No other season can compare.

In orchards, trees are bending low
With bright red apples all aglow,
The harvest time as seasons blend
And Autumn smiles at Summer's end,
My heart then shares a dream sublime –
I grasp and hold one moment's time.

Garnett Ann Schultz

*Sing to the Lord, all the
earth, announce His
salvation, day after day.*
1 Chronicles 16:23

55

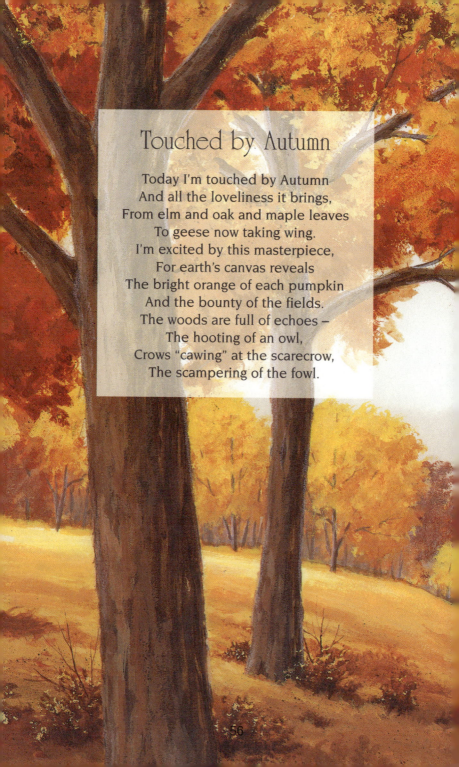

Touched by Autumn

Today I'm touched by Autumn
And all the loveliness it brings,
From elm and oak and maple leaves
To geese now taking wing.
I'm excited by this masterpiece,
For earth's canvas reveals
The bright orange of each pumpkin
And the bounty of the fields.
The woods are full of echoes –
The hooting of an owl,
Crows "cawing" at the scarecrow,
The scampering of the fowl.

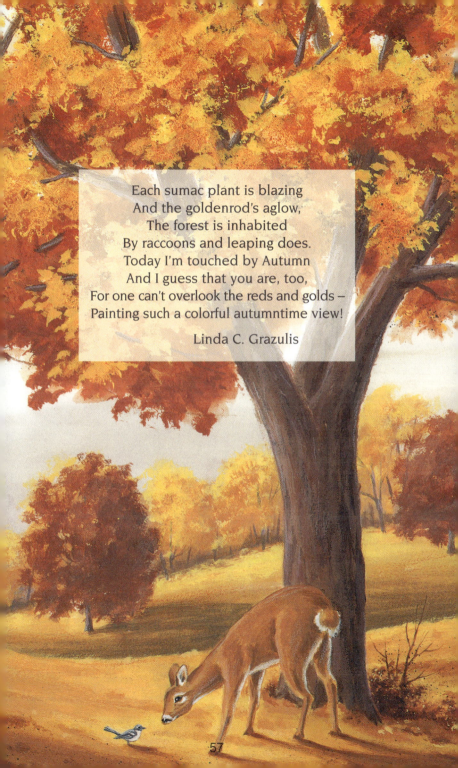

Each sumac plant is blazing
And the goldenrod's aglow,
The forest is inhabited
By raccoons and leaping does.
Today I'm touched by Autumn
And I guess that you are, too,
For one can't overlook the reds and golds –
Painting such a colorful autumntime view!

Linda C. Grazulis

God's Window of Promises

What a welcome change this is –
Such a sunny, balmy day!
Although it's stormy February,
Could early Spring be on its way?
Just a little weather window
God's provided for us to see
That Winter and its wintry ways
Very soon will have to flee!
Perhaps your life is all a storm
With good days now not in view,
Wondering when your trials will end –
All of life a wintry hue;
Don't you fret and worry, friend;
Know the best is yet to be,
Looking through God's promise window –
Soon some welcome change you'll see!
As promised Spring will never fail –
We find God true to all He said.
His faithful ones will surely see
Heart's desire not far ahead!

Lynn Fenimore Nuzzi

Friendships

As I go along life's pathway,
It is the friendships that enthrall;
My love returns a hundredfold –
This I treasure most of all.

There are those we meet
For just a time or two,
But if we show our love and care,
It will come right back to you.

It is so very affable
Just to smile and say, "Hello,"
While we make a lasting friendship
As about our way we go.

I never have had riches
Or gold that I could spend;
I am the richest one of all
If you will call me friend.

James Joseph Huesgen

When cares abound within me,
Your comfort gladdens my soul.
Psalm 94:19

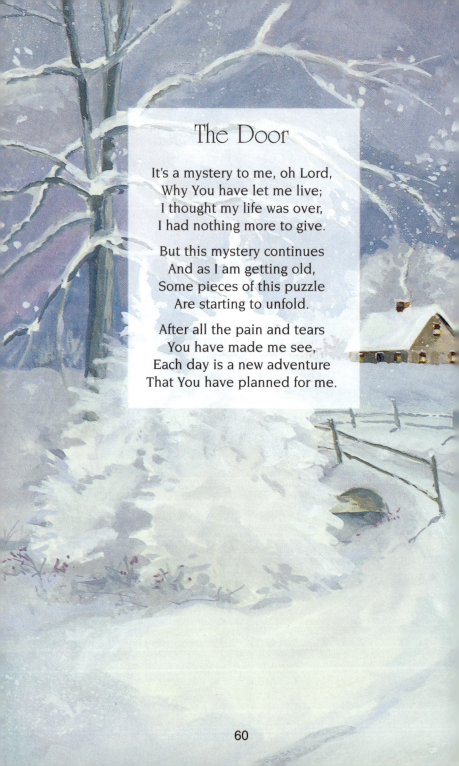

The Door

It's a mystery to me, oh Lord,
Why You have let me live;
I thought my life was over,
I had nothing more to give.

But this mystery continues
And as I am getting old,
Some pieces of this puzzle
Are starting to unfold.

After all the pain and tears
You have made me see,
Each day is a new adventure
That You have planned for me.

A new door opens every day
And I wonder what it brings –
Will my heart feel sorrow
Or will my heart have wings?

I cannot see beyond that door,
But I know You hold the key
To open up the mysteries
That lie ahead for me.

So thank You for this gift of time,
I know there's something more
You'll show me in my future,
Beyond my special door.

R. Zielinski

Who Is Listening?

Who is listening when I pray,
Whatever hour of night or day?
Who guides me on my way of life
Through moments fraught with care and strife,
On city street or country lane,
Regardless of the sun or rain?

Who is listening? Tell me, please,
As I would pause in Summer's breeze,
'Neath the skies of fairest blue,
Tender wishes – tried and true,
Looking to the heavens fair,
Moment spent in quiet prayer...

Times I've spent so oft alone,
Dreaming dreams so much my own,
Faith and courage ever mine.
Always hope and peace sublime,
As each path I fondly trod...
Who is listening? Only God.

Garnett Ann Schultz

Wonderful Wintertime

Beneath a sky of cobalt blue,
The day is wrapped in Winter's hue.
Diamond-sparkled snowflakes fly
Like frost-kissed magic from on high.

Colorful blue jays brave and bold
Hop around and loudly scold.
Cardinals decorate the scene
On snowy boughs of evergreen.

Icy winds sculpt drifts of white
And etch each silver-frosted night.
December hangs her frozen head
And sleeps upon an ermine bed.

Nora M. Bozeman

You fixed all the limits of the land;
Summer and Winter You made.
Psalm 74:17

God's
Wintertime Wonders

Snow feathers sail the silvered sky
As glistening snowbirds flutter by;
The pine trees gleam with shimmering frost,
Near lakes with powdered sugar tossed.

In brisk, cold winds of the ice-trimmed world,
Nature's frost-flowers swing and swirl,
Dazzling diamonds sparkle on fir trees of green,
Soft moonbeams glow on Winter's crystal sheen.

Through filigrees of frost-fringed lace,
A thousand jewels glimmer in place,
The harmony of Heaven shines from hills above
To reflect God's message of hope, peace and love.

Winter's breathless beauty in skyward sweeps,
From snowy valleys to frozen rivers deep,
We share in grandeur our God's majestic land –
God holds creation's marvels in His wondrous hand.

Elisabeth Weaver Winstead

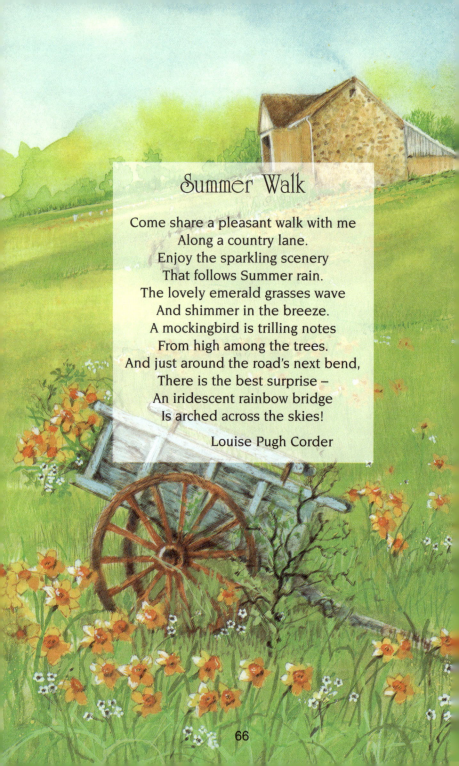

Summer Walk

Come share a pleasant walk with me
Along a country lane.
Enjoy the sparkling scenery
That follows Summer rain.
The lovely emerald grasses wave
And shimmer in the breeze.
A mockingbird is trilling notes
From high among the trees.
And just around the road's next bend,
There is the best surprise –
An iridescent rainbow bridge
Is arched across the skies!

Louise Pugh Corder

Simple Gifts

Of all the gifts you've given me,
The one I cherish most
Is that which comes straight from your heart...
As pure as Heaven's host.

You fill my cup with happiness...
Each day more love you show...
As constant and as timeless
As the river's waters flow.

And we've only just begun,
As each new day unfolds...
More precious joys and rapture,
More memories to have and hold.

I hunger for the future
With no fear of growing old.
You are what dreams are made of...
Your love lights up my soul.

Marilyn C. Hinson

*Fill us at daybreak with
Your love, that all our
days we may sing for joy.*
Psalm 90:14

A Rainy Season

This has been a rainy season,
Clouds have surely come our way,
All are waiting for the sunshine
To put on a grand display.
It is springtime in the country
And a harvest to renew,
We must sow the seeds for planting
For the harvest to come through.
God, our Father, up in Heaven
Knows exactly what it takes
And He sends the rain and sunshine,
For He never makes mistakes.
When the clouds up in the heavens
Roll along, "come into view,"
Be assured the sun will follow
As He sends this blessing, too.

Katherine Smith Matheney

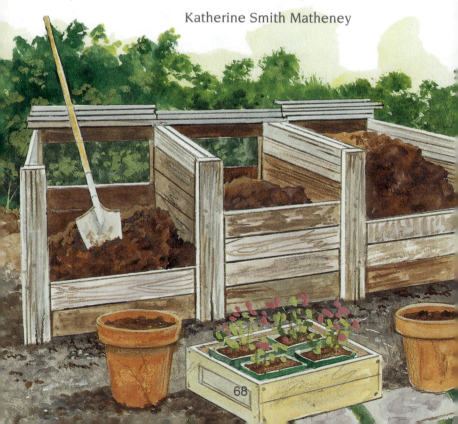

Simple Trust

Have you ever wondered how
Trees come alive in Spring…
Barren branches fill with leaves
With new buds opening?
And have you seen the crocus
Push right up through the snow?
How could it know the timing
Was right for it to show?
The lily bulb, long dormant,
In frozen, icy ground,
Awakens from its slumber
…Spreads beauty all around.
Knowing leaves will drop in Fall
…Appear again in Spring…
Shouldn't it be simple
To trust God for everything?

Anna M. Matthews

Spring Is

Spring is tulips and daffodils,
Blooming dogwoods and greening hills;
Sun-kissed skies with white clouds sailing –
Sparrows with sweet songs regaling.
Spring is splashing brooks and streams,
Waterfalls and bright moonbeams;
Golden days, star-studded nights –
Spectacular sunset's flaming lights.
Spring is priceless and inspiring,
Overwhelming and beguiling;
Her lavish beauty electrifies –
And spins a spell before my eyes.

Nora M. Bozeman

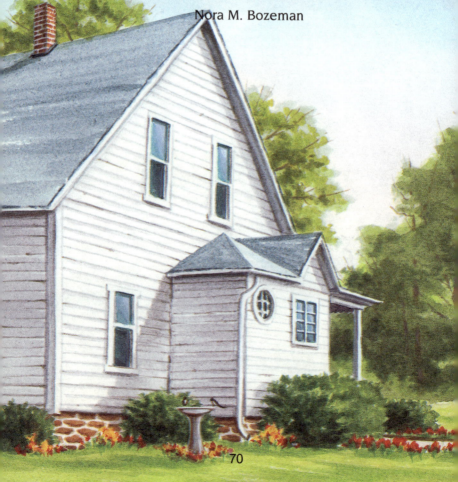

Rejoice!

Rejoice, Summer is upon us.
The earth's now green and lush.
Fragrances of the season
Have arrived in quite a hush.

We now alight the charcoal
And put sunscreen on the face.
We manicure our lovely lawns
And plant the garden at our place.

A pleasantly soft evening breeze
Brings music to our ears.
'Tis time to get out ball and bat
And hear the children's cheers.

It matters not just where we live,
There'll be a pink sunset,
And memories of Summers past
We lived without regret.

Henry Charles Doherty

*This is the day the Lord
has made; let us be glad
and rejoice in it.*
Psalm 118:24

71

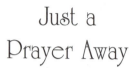

Just a
Prayer Away

God's only just a prayer away.
Oh yes, I know it's true;
And yet when trials and testings come,
What is it that I do?
I run in circles trying hard
To solve the problems, right?
But I can't find solutions, nor
A peaceful heart at night.

God is the One who holds the keys
To doors He knows are best.
He has the answers to our needs,
But we must trust and rest
In knowing God's in full control,
Performing as He should.
He'll take the problems – yours and mine,
And work them out for good.

God is our comfort in the night,
Our strength from day to day,
If we just lay our burdens down
And let Him have His way.
It's trusting, not trying, that
Brings blessings to our life
And gives us sweet content and joy
And hope that conquers strife.

I'm thankful God forgives us when
We wander from His side,
And gently leads us back again
In His will to abide.
So now when storm clouds hide the sun
And new trials come my way,
On bended knee I'll go to Him
Who's just a prayer away.

Beverly J. Anderson

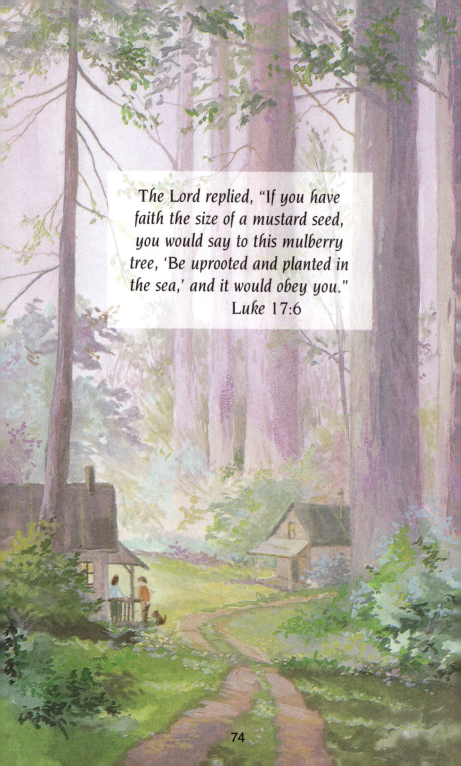

The Lord replied, "If you have faith the size of a mustard seed, you would say to this mulberry tree, 'Be uprooted and planted in the sea,' and it would obey you."

Luke 17:6

My Faith

Even though the winds of fate
Blow sorrow into my life,
I know my God is merciful
And will help me through my strife.

How good He is to love me so,
And all that He asks of me
Is to love my neighbor as myself
And to love Him willingly.

God put a claim on my heart
And filled it with His love;
The faith that I am filled with
Is a gift from Him above.

Now as I walk this earthly sod,
God sends me His loving grace
To keep me on the right path
Through the faith that I embrace.

Shirley Hile Powell

The Little Things

Lord, teach me to be thankful for
The little things in life,
The little joys we oft o'erlook
Amid the daily strife.

The first sweet rose in early June –
Face washed with morning dew,
The laughter of a little child
That warms the heart of you.

Lord, in the rush of daily chores,
Bid me to pause awhile
To linger in the sunshine of
A neighbor's friendly smile.

And let me not be so involved
That I would fail to see
A robin teach her young to fly
And miss such ecstasy.

Sometimes a gift of joy is in
A little helpful deed
Or kindly word that someone offers
In our time of need.

Teach me, O Lord, to live each day
Above my meager self,
Ever thankful for the little things
More precious than all wealth.

Kay Hoffman

*Give thanks to the Lord,
for He is good, for His
kindness endures forever.*
1 Chronicles 16:34

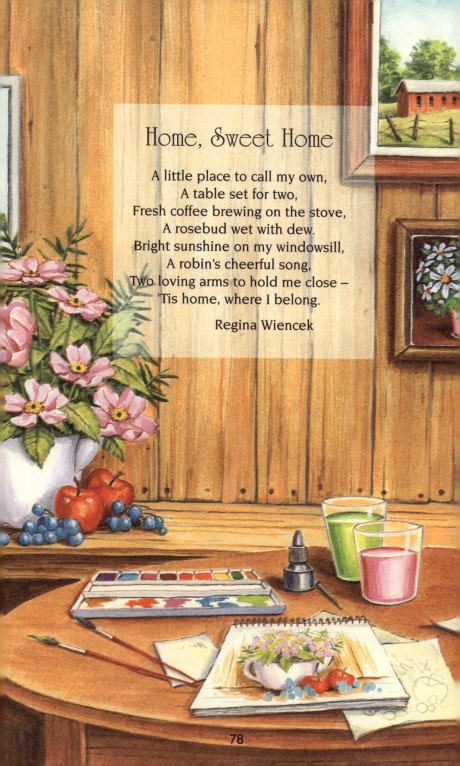

Home, Sweet Home

A little place to call my own,
A table set for two,
Fresh coffee brewing on the stove,
A rosebud wet with dew.
Bright sunshine on my windowsill,
A robin's cheerful song,
Two loving arms to hold me close –
'Tis home, where I belong.

Regina Wiencek

August Is a Copper Kettle

August is a copper kettle
Filled to brim with molten sun;
Pouring golden batter slowly
Till its griddlecakes are done.

August is a desert nomad
Traveling through an arid land,
Searching for some small oasis
In an endless stretch of sand!

August is a dreamer's knapsack
Packed with lazy, leisure days,
Strapped to Summer's sturdy shoulders
With the "chords" time's piper plays.

August, stay a while longer,
Let your heat becalm us all;
There are duties waiting for us
In the workplace of the Fall!

John C. Bonser

Nature's Fashion Shop

I'm going to stroll through the meadow
And visit wildflowers in bloom;
Their presence, how sweet and inspiring;
They are always so fresh and well-groomed.

I'm always amazed at their colors
Created in lavish design
That suits each one to perfection,
Far exceeding these tatters of mine.

Let each of us learn to be trustful
And we shall appear bright and new,
For when we've grown firm in God's graces,
He'll fashion our own wardrobe, too.

But first we must truly be trusting
And convinced of His infinite care
For Him to apply His keen needle
In preparing the garments we wear.

Don Beckman

Summertime Designs

The wind whispers to the willows,
Soft breezes caress the trees;
The perfumed scents of Summer
Gently waft on the sunburned breeze.

Days are gift-wrapped in radiance
And delicate marigolds;
Gardens host dew-dropped roses
And a bluebird who loudly scolds.

The gems of August dwindle down
As Autumn intertwines,
'Round the glorious, golden days
That summertime designs.

Nora M. Bozeman

Come, Walk With Me

Come, walk with me along the way
Where lanes are Autumn-dressed.
Come, drink in all the colors fair
And let your heart be blessed.

Come, see the flaming sumac plumes
Lift banners to the sky
As goldenrod and asters nod
To us as we pass by.

Come, walk with me when leaves turn gold
And hills wear crimson hue,
Where pumpkins grow in amber fields
'Neath sky of matchless blue.

Come, walk with me this misty morn;
There's splendor to behold;
Along the country lanes we'll see
God's miracles unfold.

Beverly J. Anderson

His Touch

I see silos in the distance
Among the leaves of red and gold.
I look in awe and wonder
As I see God's touch unfold.

As I travel down life's highway,
I see Him everywhere.
I'm on the road to Heaven
And I see His touch so fair.

The mountains that I've had to climb
Grow straight beneath my feet,
As I look ahead and see Him there,
My Savior, oh, so sweet.

Dona M. Maroney

You, Lord, are just in all Your ways,
faithful in all Your works.
Psalm 145:17

Autumn,
Dear Autumn

Autumn, dear Autumn,
You're off on your spree.
There are so many auras.
You beckon to me.

The rustling wind noises,
The falling of leaves,
The joy and the gladness
One's heart receives.

Tent cities of cornstalks
Tied neatly in rows,
The wind and the trees
In Autumn's last throes.

There's cider and pumpkins
And colors galore,
Parcels of folks
In each country store.

Thanksgiving is due,
Life is such bliss,
Nothing I've ventured
Is sweeter than this.

James Joseph Huesgen

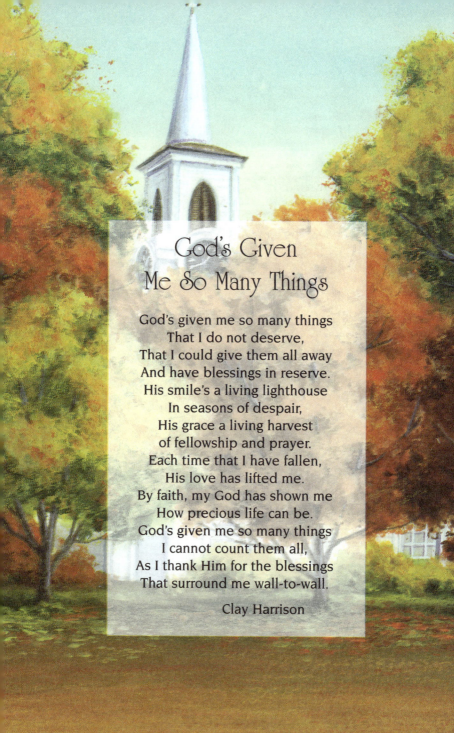

God's Given
Me So Many Things

God's given me so many things
That I do not deserve,
That I could give them all away
And have blessings in reserve.
His smile's a living lighthouse
In seasons of despair,
His grace a living harvest
of fellowship and prayer.
Each time that I have fallen,
His love has lifted me.
By faith, my God has shown me
How precious life can be.
God's given me so many things
I cannot count them all,
As I thank Him for the blessings
That surround me wall-to-wall.

Clay Harrison

Keep Singing

On waking in the morning,
The birds sing merrily...
The robins, wrens and cardinals,
The sparrows in the lea.
If raindrops pitter-patter
Or sunshine comes along,
The birds are always singing,
They always have a song.

They know not what the day brings,
What snares may lie ahead;
Unlike us human beings,
They're never known to fret.
They just keep on a-singing
From early morn till night;
How following their example
Would make our days so bright!

Loise Pinkerton Fritz

*I will sing to the Lord as
long as I live; I will sing
praise to my God while I
have my being.*
Psalm 104:33

Dancing Sunbeams

If sunbeams dance on Autumn leaves,
If colors flare in light –
If shadows move with random ease
Then disappear from sight…

To come again, as if perforce,
As partners in a dance –
If leaves of brown and red and gold
Must miss autumnal chance…

To boast full shadings for kind eye
Of suitors of the Fall –
If dry and dusty winds of fate
Bid Autumn make its call…

Then one more day of dappled light
Upon a fallen leaf –
September goes; October comes –
Perverse this sudden thief.

If in a chilling moment when
The skies turn ashen gray –
If sunbeams dance on falling leaves –
Then Summer's gone away.

Henry W. Gurley

The wind goeth toward the south,
and turneth about unto the north;
it whirleth about continually, and the wind
returneth again according to His circuits.
Ecclesiastes 1:6

Winter

The icy hand of Winter
Captured the wayward breeze.
Its fingers seemed reluctant
To tender a release.
It clutched near the windowpane,
It hovered 'round the door.
Every time I ventured out,
It gripped tighter than before.
Its digits tingled down my spine,
Chilling to the bone.
Often, when I looked outside,
I thanked God for my home.

Ruth J. Tabberer

*Ice and snow, bless the
Lord; praise and exalt
Him above all forever.*
Daniel 3:70

Heart Gifts

It means so very much to me
To go to God in prayer;
Whose works beyond all humankind,
Whose love is everywhere!

My Father, God, is always near
Whenever I'm in need;
Because He knows 'tis only He
Who makes my life succeed!

Oh, Father, God, who art my own,
I'll never from Thee part;
For I shall always grateful be
For gift of happy heart!

Sancie Earman King

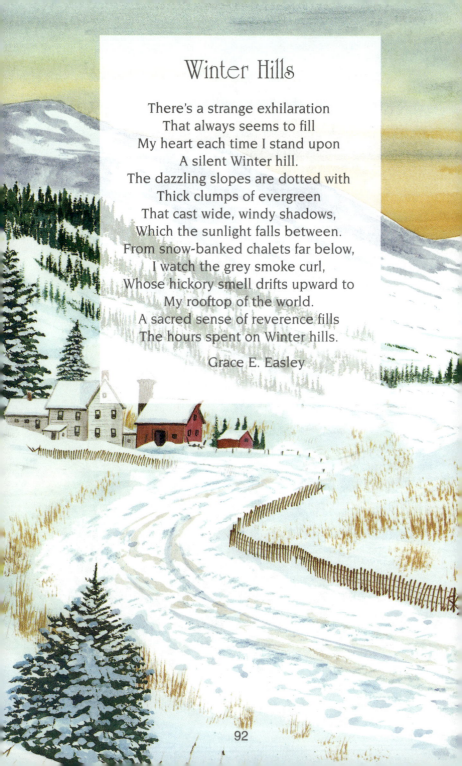

Winter Hills

There's a strange exhilaration
That always seems to fill
My heart each time I stand upon
A silent Winter hill.
The dazzling slopes are dotted with
Thick clumps of evergreen
That cast wide, windy shadows,
Which the sunlight falls between.
From snow-banked chalets far below,
I watch the grey smoke curl,
Whose hickory smell drifts upward to
My rooftop of the world.
A sacred sense of reverence fills
The hours spent on Winter hills.

Grace E. Easley

A Winter Day

It's the last day of Winter
And the snow's falling down
In a pattern of beauty,
Not making a sound.

It's a sight to behold and
Such a beautiful scene
With a lovely, white blanket,
It's a wintertime dream.

Oh, I love sights of Winter –
Snow-capped mountains so high,
Heavy, snow-laden pine trees –
That's a treat to the eye.

God the Artist has chosen
For this canvas-type dream
Lovely blankets of snowflakes
For this rare Winter scene.

Katherine Smith Matheney

First Snow

It is a time that I love so
When comes the first of season's snow;
And down a country lane I go
In Winter's sheer delight.

The holly leaves in beauty pose
With berries redder than a rose –
And is that frost that tweaks my nose
As sunset bows to night?

I see some tracks – were rabbits here?
For in the brush they disappear;
I wonder if they left in fear
To burrows out of sight?

It is this time which brings me cheer,
A season that I cherish dear;
A special fragment of my year –
I love this world of white!

Henry W. Gurley

Snowflakes From Heaven

Sometime during the hush of the night,
Earth put on her wintry white face.
The sparkle of fresh snowflakes
Veiled the ground like bridal lace.

The fir trees hung low in the distance –
Green boughs pushing through delicate white.
A redbird perched high on the mailbox flag
Added a flair to the heavenly sight.

Animals were everywhere, searching for food,
A raccoon was first on the scene;
And a chubby, new snowman stood on the hill,
Wearing a top hat with a silky, black sheen.

I felt such laughter, sprinkled with tears,
Looking back on many a Winter before,
When snowflakes slipped from the hand of God
And floated down, like a gift, to my door!

Barbara Cagle Ray

Of a Woodland Scene

So gray the sky and dismal,
And the rain is falling near;
All creatures seeking shelter now;
How can they disappear?

What primal urge tells them to flee?
And where must they all go?
And look! The rain is changing to
A lace-like, falling snow.

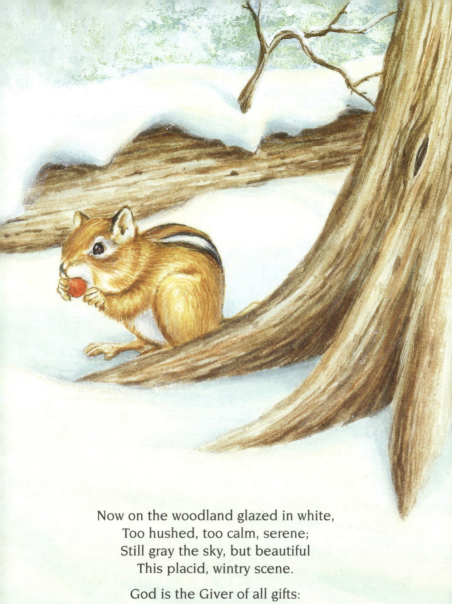

Now on the woodland glazed in white,
Too hushed, too calm, serene;
Still gray the sky, but beautiful
This placid, wintry scene.

God is the Giver of all gifts:
His sky of leaden gray –
His creatures seeking shelter and
A special Winter day.

Henry W. Gurley

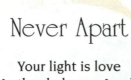

Never Apart

Your light is love
In the darkness, Lord,
It's with me night and day.
It's with me when I'm with You
And with me when I stray.

The light of Your love
Fills me with joy
And happiness divine.
I know Your love is mine, dear Lord,
Until the end of time.

Where'er I go
I feel Your love,
It's locked deep within my heart.
And I know, no matter where I am,
We will never be apart.

Dona M. Maroney

Never Alone

I never feel alone because
I have a Friend who's near;
He knows me like no other one,
To me He's ever dear.
He tells me that I'm special,
He gave His life for me;
I pray that in this life I live
I'll always faithful be.
This Friend I found in Jesus
I'd like to share with you,
But you must open your heart's door
As I was led to do.
When you ask Jesus to come in
You will never be the same
And you'll never be alone
When you call upon His name.
I walked a path with downcast heart,
My day was filled with dread,
Needing strength beyond my own,
Unto my Lord I plead.
I told Him of my heartache,
The anguish I'd been through
When a friend that I loved dearly
Had proved to be untrue.
So gently then He whispered,
"My child, I understand."
It was then that I noticed
The nailprint on His hand.

Kay Hoffman

The Barefoot
Days of Childhood

The barefoot days of childhood
Bring memories divine
Of adventures in Mom's garden
When I was eight and nine.

We never had much money,
But we were rich, you see,
For Mom's hollyhocks and roses
Meant more than gold to me.

Bright hummingbirds and bumblebees
Came to play at will,
And there were always bluebirds
Singing on the hill.

Sweet marigolds and zinnias
Were quite a sight to see,
Growing wild across the meadow
In rainbow harmony.

Some might call me sentimental,
But that's O.K., you see,
For the barefoot days of childhood
Are gifts God gave to me!

Clay Harrison

Oh, the depth of the
riches and wisdom and
knowledge of God!
Romans 11:33

Spring Treasures

My heart overflows with happiness
Now that Spring is in the air.
The barren fields have turned to green
And the trees are no longer bare.

Sometimes I must catch my breath
Seeing the beauty this season brings.
Everything is so fresh and alive.
Birds have their new songs to sing.

Colorful and fragrant flowers
Fill an artist with utter delight.
It is God's time of renewal.
Things are so beautiful and bright.

Lord, I thank Thee for the springtime
That gives me such joy and pleasure.
It's just another of Your gifts
That You gave to me to treasure.

Shirley Hile Powell

Breath of Spring

Those golden hues light up the day
And beckon all to come along
To welcome back the breath of Spring
That's cradled in each robin's song.

A crocus nods her pretty head
And brushes dewdrop from her gown,
She bids the daffodils stand tall –
No need in Spring to wear a frown.

The little woodland creatures scurry,
Alive and grateful for the sun
That warms their hearts and makes it easy
To see that daily chores are done.

There is no other time nor season
When life renews and makes hearts glow.
Give thanks for every sunlit morning
And praise the One who makes it so.

Shirley Takacs

*I will give thanks to You, O Lord,
with all my heart; I will declare
all Your wondrous deeds.*
Psalm 9:2

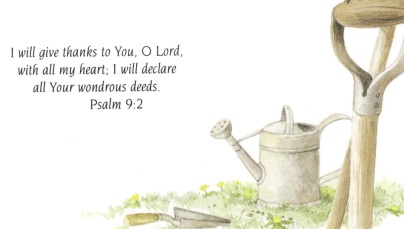

I'm Overjoyed It's Springtime

I'm overjoyed it's springtime
'Cause new birth sprouts here and there,
Butterflies show off new wings
And meadows grow a green carpet everywhere.

The crocus throws off its snowy blanket
As daffodils begin to shine.
Around the wooden arbor,
Sprawling vines entwine.

The babbling brooks dance faster
And the old mill picks up speed,
The forest blooms profusely
With rhododendrons and with weeds.

The sound of children's laughter
Echoes loud and clear
And in the distance can be spotted
A family of white-tailed deer.

I'm so overjoyed it's springtime
And I hope that you are, too.
Out of love God created happy moments
And skies of springtime blue!

Linda C. Grazulis

*My lips shall shout for joy
as I sing Your praises.*
Psalm 71:23

The Lighthouse

The lighthouse stands against the storm,
Beside an angry sea
And sends a beacon, soft and warm,
For fearful ships to see.

Waves crash like thunder on the rocks
As winds begin to wail,
But the keeper of the lighthouse
Fears not the raging gale.

He's weathered many storms before
On dark and lonely nights
And guided safely to the shore
Lost ships that saw his light.

Our God is like that lighthouse,
A Beacon in the night
Who guides lost souls to the shore
With His redeeming light!

Clay Harrison

My Best

Many times I sit alone
And think of days gone by,
The days I spent away back home…
How swiftly time does fly.

If I could live those days again,
Turn back the pages of time,
I'd change a lot of things, it seems,
Within this heart of mine.

But since I cannot time erase,
Nor live it o'er again,
I'll do my best from day to day
To fill redemption's plan.

For He has formed a pattern
To guide me every day;
So I must follow closely
My Guide along the way.

Then when 'tis all completed
At setting of the sun,
I'll hear my Heavenly Father say,
"Well done, My child, well done."

Helen Humbarger

Stepping-Stones

In everything, be patient,
For good shall follow bad
And in time you won't remember
Most problems that you had.

In everything, show kindness
For others' great concerns,
And, my friend, it will amaze you
How great are your returns!

In everything, be willing
To learn, endure and grow,
For a candle that's unlighted
Cannot begin to glow!

In everything, show courage,
For courage conquers fear,
And fear can cloud our judgment
When storms of life appear.

In everything, be thankful,
For each path we must trod
Shall become a stepping-stone
Which leads the soul to God!

Clay Harrison

Love is patient,
love is kind...
1 Corinthians 13:4

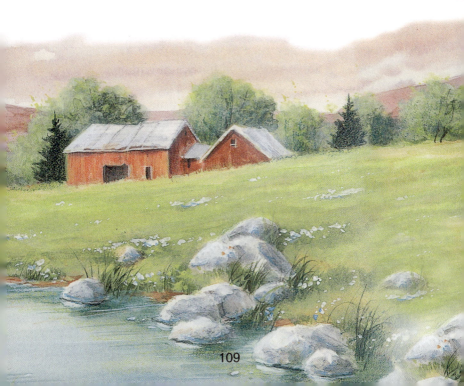

Tranquility

Take time away from daily chores
To capture moments sweet,
Enjoying happy, sun-filled days
When life is more complete,
To pause beneath the maple tree
And find each blessing real,
The meadow vast where children play
In happiness ideal.
Take time to capture Summer dreams,
Then tuck them fast away
So very deep within your heart
For one so far-off day.
Summer is a tranquil time,
A time of peace and bliss,
With cotton clouds in skies above
And Nature's loving kiss.
The world is such a busy place,
Hours steal away life's fun,
While daily chores are always there
Still waiting to be done,
And yet the moments that we spend
With Nature – bright and free,
To walk a magic country lane
And find tranquility.

Garnett Ann Schultz

Letting Go

Why is it that I always think
That my way is the best?
Why can't I look beyond myself
And on God's shoulders rest?

Why does my stubborn nature
Want to do things its own way?
God tries so hard to teach me,
But I often go astray.

I really want to listen,
But the world's call is so strong…
It often overshadows Him,
It tempts me to belong.

But if I want His perfect peace,
I must let go of "me"
And trust in Him for guidance…
Then I'll find victory.

Frances Gregory Pasch

111

Blessings Upon Blessings

Blessings upon blessings
God sends from above
That tell of His mercy
And unfailing love.

The air that we breathe
And the food that we eat,
Strength afresh for each day,
Our tasks to complete.

With sunshine and flowers,
He brightens life's way,
Sends cheery birdsongs,
Children's laughter so gay.

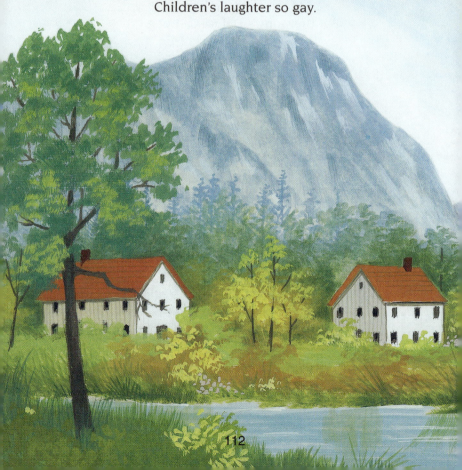

Our family and home,
The friends we hold dear,
He gives us His promise
He'll ever walk near.

All that we call "ours"
He so graciously gives,
We should praise Him and thank Him
Each day we live.

For tender His mercy
And great is His Love;
Our cup runneth over
With gifts from above.

Kay Hoffman

Gifts Sublime

God gave me more gifts today
Than I can comprehend,
For every single moment,
His blessings does He send.
He gave me gold at daybreak
When the sun peeked through the skies,
Wafted beauty 'bout the yard
On wings of butterflies.
God gave me rest at noonday
'Neath shade of towering trees,
Dropped dainty, purple violets
Upon the country leas.
God gave me some cool water
And food on which to sup,
More and more with gifts sublime
He filled my earthly cup.
God gave me more gifts today
Than I can comprehend,
But most of all His tender love,
Which daily does He send.

Virginia Borman Grimmer

Song
Without End

Slate-blue swallows soaring over,
Flowering peach trees all aglow,
Roadside daisies and purple clover,
Slim willows wave in pale-green row.

Ripe fields of corn and sun-gold bees,
Quiet, tawny cows in meadows graze,
Bright robins in the cherry trees
With ceaseless song God's glories praise.

Elisabeth Weaver Winstead

*I will praise the name of God
in song, and I will glorify
Him with thanksgiving.*
Psalm 69:31

115

Sow Seeds of Love

Sow seeds of love along life's road
Wherever you might travel;
However heavy be your load,
Let pleasant dreams unravel.
These simple miracles so sweet
Can fill your heart with gladness;
Regardless who you chance to meet,
You'll never know a sadness.

Seeds of love will blossom forth
Beneath soft skies of blue
To lend a sunshine to the earth
When Winter days are through.
A friendly smile will be your own,
A kindly word – a touch,
True happiness you've never known
That offers, oh, so much.

Do plant your garden day by day
With magic seeds of caring,
Take time for work, yet time for play
And always time for sharing.
So precious is each breaking dawn,
Look up to God above,
You'll know a peace when day is gone
While sowing seeds of love.

Garnett Ann Schultz

*...sow your seed and then
water it by hand, as in a
vegetable garden.*
Deuteronomy 11:10

117

Fall Foliage

The trees around the lake
Adorned in shades of Fall –
In crimson, rust and yellow,
Standing so straight and tall.

Adorned in the colors of Autumn,
Reflecting all of their glory,
Shining down into the lake,
Telling Mother Nature's story.

And further on along the road
Were trees still dressed in green,
Refusing to be hurried
In Autumn colors to be seen.

The landscape was breathtaking,
Spreading out over the land –
The work of a Master Artist
With a very loving hand.

Erna Gwillim

What Color Is Autumn?

What color is Autumn?
I really can't tell –
Sometimes it is golden,
I know it so well,
And then very suddenly
To my surprise,
It changes to auburn
In front of my eyes.
What color is nature
This late Autumn day?
There's a whirlwind of orange
In the leaves as they play,
But no – some are brown
Or a crimson would seem,
But there in the valley,
A trace still of green.
What color October?
My dear, can't you tell,
'Tis a rainbow of beauty
Where Autumn doth dwell.
The green and the golden,
The crimson and brown…
You'll find Autumn's colors
In leaves falling down.

Garnett Ann Schultz

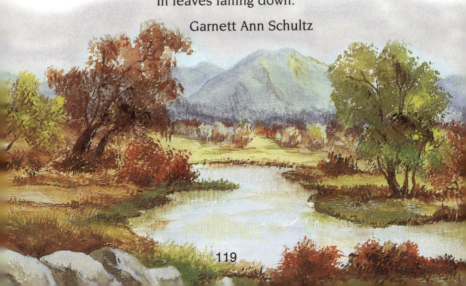

Roads

Roads have such enticing ways
To lure you 'round a bend
Where there are often lovely scenes –
Surprises without end.

Roads wander with a woodland stream
Or curl around a shore
And crawl up to a mountaintop,
Then back to where before.

With sunbeams they play hide-and-seek
Where the foliage isn't dense,
Then skip across a meadowland
Where the flowers are the fence.

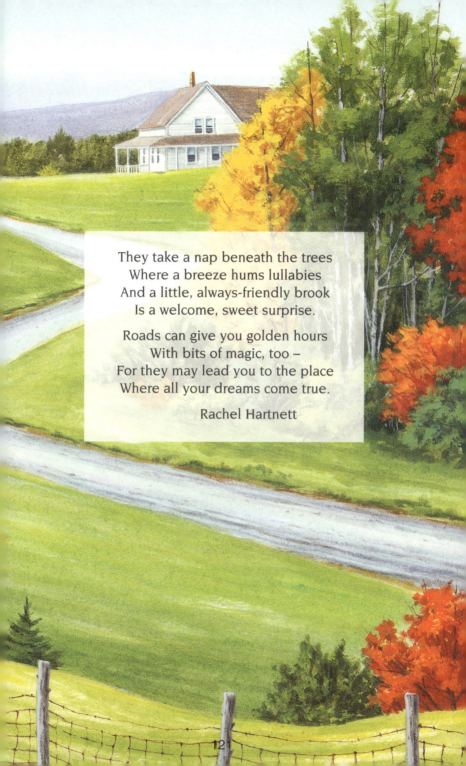

They take a nap beneath the trees
Where a breeze hums lullabies
And a little, always-friendly brook
Is a welcome, sweet surprise.

Roads can give you golden hours
With bits of magic, too –
For they may lead you to the place
Where all your dreams come true.

Rachel Hartnett

The Master Painter

Beyond my windowpane I see
God's lacy snowflakes silently
Descend and paint an artist's scene,
All glistening white and so serene.
And as I gaze with rapt delight,
My heart is quickened by the sight
Of sparkling "diamonds" in the snow,
Transforming all with Heaven's glow.
With certainty and joy I know
The Master Painter made it so.

Vi B. Chevalier

*Let them give thanks to the Lord for
His kindness and His wondrous
deeds to the children of men.*
Psalm 107:8

We Are the Same

We live in different places
And we walk on different ways –
With different styles and modes of life,
At labor and at play,
But we are all the very same
In hopes and dreams we pray,
And ask – the same – of Jesus Christ
Upon our Judgment Day.
For we are children of the Lord
And kin to common needs
That fill us with the loves of life
That are of Christian creed;
And this is as it's meant to be –
To make our lives sublime –
For all your dreams of love and life
Are just the same as mine.

Michael Dubina

Winter Etchings

The morning light brought true delight,
A time when snow was falling.
I can feel the child within me yet
And Winters past were calling.

The children played within the snow,
Old folks stayed near the fire.
To be young and nimble was my wish,
A long, heartfelt desire.

The birdbath was a mushroom,
There was a whirring all around.
As a wind blew snow upon the roof,
A white fan came swishing down.

Everything had turned to sculptures
And soon I'd shovel to the gate
Where children looked like snowmen
As the day was getting late.

And then I cozied by the fire
Where I would sip a warming brew
As a wind came whipping at the house
To help the drafts come through.

Like so many other Winters,
This one, too, would hold a past
With so many stories stowed away,
I knew this one, too, would last.

James Joseph Huesgen

He spreads snow like wool;
frost He strews like ashes.
Psalm 147:16

Winter's Promise

As Winter laid her ermine wrap,
Embracing the earth below,
The trees bowed in reverence
And the bushes curtsied low.

I looked upon this glorious sight
And knew there'd never be
A single stroke of an artist's brush
To equal this beauty I see!

And just when this blanket of beauty
Succumbed to the sun's warm rays,
The warmth and the chill collided
And the earth shed its ermine for haze.

The Creator had taken His magical brush
And bathed my soul with His art.
"Enjoy it, My child… no price is attached,
It's My gift to believing hearts!"

Suddenly, I knew it was all so true,
His plan to redeem the world;
We'd all be made new with a stroke of His brush
As surely as Spring is unfurled!

Doris Wallace

...The Lord, your God will
bless you as He promised.
Deuteronomy 15:6

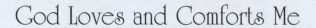

God Loves and Comforts Me

As quiet as the stars I sat
In darkness of the night
And watched the moon climb up the sky
'Til early morning light:
I knew that God did make it all –
Declared it good and right.

Another day I sat me down
Beside a rivulet
As it tripped merrily downstream –
In thought I hear it yet.

Another time I sat alone
Beneath an old oak tree
And felt a breeze caress my face
And that reminded me
That God is always by my side
To keep and comfort me.

Luther Elvis Albright